ROOTS & BULBS

PURE

JUICING FOR LIFE

SARAH CADJI

PHOTOGRAPHY BY KRISTIN PERERS

Quadrille
PUBLISHING

CONTENTS

INTRODUCTION

THE RAW VEGETABLE FOOD REGIME IS THE MOST
POTENT, CONCENTRATED AND NUTRIENT RICH WAY
OF LIFE FOR HUMAN BEINGS. A WAY OF LIVING
THAT IS SIMPLE, CONTROLLABLE AND CLEAN.

I grew up in Athens, Greece, where the weather is warm throughout the year, with no harsh winters and an incredible climate that enables fresh produce to grow naturally. As a child, my grandmother and I would always buy our fresh food from stalls in the market, where we held conversations with the farmers who grew the produce themselves. We always had a very personal relationship with the food that we put inside our bodies.

In my twenties, I moved to London and started working in finance. Life was great: I was productive, surviving in a big city all by myself and creating a life that was all mine. I was constantly rushing around trying to get everything done, without leaving any time to think about the choices I was making about my diet and my long-term health. Inevitably my body, gave way and I crashed. I started waking up exhausted, feeling nauseous throughout the day and more importantly I started feeling depressed. I had no energy to get out of bed in the mornings and I felt my body had turned into a lifeless piece of matter.

I went to tens of doctors who prescribed medicine, which I refused to take. Eventually, I decided to take matters into my own hands. I tried to be rational and reasonable and use my common sense and give my way of life a lot of thought. It became very clear to me that if I wanted to get better and feel different, I would need a long-term solution. I looked at my lifestyle, my eating habits, my exercise routine and I realised I had never properly considered the impact what I put inside my body on a daily basis was having on my wellbeing. I had to do something about it. This was my life and if I didn't look out for myself, I would never be able to carve my own path. My health journey had started.

I studied hundreds of diets, I read various books about food and ingredients and I met a lot of experts in the field of medicine and nutrition. One common thread that weaved throughout all of my findings and has now become my golden rule 'a 'raw vegetable-based diet prevents and resolves body deficiencies and lack of nutrient-based illnesses in our world today'.

I realised I needed to focus on the benefits of raw, green and leafy vegetables; as organic and locally sourced produce contains at least twice the nutritional mineral content of regular produce. The raw vegetable food regime is the most potent, concentrated and nutrient rich way of life for human beings. A way of living that is simple, controllable and clean.

I started thinking about 'balance' and how essential it is to live a long, healthy life. The key was to find a way of eating more greens and the rest in moderation. I recognised the power of adding in the good stuff, instead of taking out the bad. There simply isn't any sustainability in crash juice diets, instead it is all about finding a way of juicing every day and finding your own 'balance'.

I was making and drinking fresh, raw and organic vegetable juice every day, whilst carefully analysing my other food choices. I used nutritional common sense and exercised balance. After a year, I was alert, focused and happy. Vegetable juices were feeding my body with intense concentrated nutrition and it was all down to the choices I had made. I felt so empowered, ready to take on the world with an inner strength that could not be measured.

This is what a consistent, balanced approach to your health will do for you too. The healing powers of raw juicing are too many to mention, but if I can do it, you can do it. Juicing makes your daily diet more understandable and much more manageable. Raw vegetable juicing is so self-explanatory, all you need is a willingness to try and the courage to take the leap that will guarantee you a better life.

I went on to leave my finance job and open the first vegetable and organic juice and food bar 'Roots & Bulbs' in London. We own two of them now and are on our way to open our third store this year. I have never in my life felt better, more healthy, clean and more importantly happy.

I know you can get there too, all I want to do is show you how easy it is. I can't wait to start this journey with you.

Sarah

ROOTS & BULBS

JUICING: THE BASICS

JUICING FOR LIFE

So, you have heard about juicing and how it can change your life, make you skinnier, give you a healthy, natural boost and dramatically change your life for the better. You have decided to give it a go, but you don't really know where to start or more importantly – how and what to juice...

This introduction is filled with the most important principles of juicing. Hopefully, it will kick-start your eagerness and your willingness to begin juicing for life. Let's start!

VEGETABLES & FRUITS

Fresh vegetables and fruits are the basis of any healthy diet as they are the source of nearly every nutrient the human body requires for optimum function. But fruit juice won't help you feel better or heal your body. This doesn't mean that fruit isn't good for you, it is, but it has too much sugar. Drinking fruit juice will result in having an internal insulin spike, which will leave your body craving more sweet food or liquid.

Instead, we should be drinking vegetable juices which have a small amount of fruit in them. Green vegetable juices are essential to establishing a healthy body and immune system. They build your internal system and strengthen your blood. They are very high in calcium, magnesium, iron, potassium, phosphorus, zinc and vitamins A,C,E and K. They are also loaded with folic acid and chlorophyll and purify the blood, prevent diseases, improve circulation, strengthen your immune system and boost your energy levels. Clearly, the facts speak for themselves, vegetable juices are superior to fruit juices. Allowing a bit of fruit in your juices and smoothies is fine and will help your palate turn greener and healthier. But be careful, never add more than one or two fruits inside your juice, as it's simply too much sugar.

It is always better to eat your fruit and drink your vegetables. Fruits eaten, contain the fibre which will slow down the release of sugar into your body, whereas juiced vegetables will release all the goodness and essential missing vitamins quickly back into your body, without insulin spikes.

JUICING YOUR VEGETABLES

Why juice your vegetables? The answer is very simple: it's all to do with how quickly the nutrients reach your body. Solid foods such as a carrot or a big chunk of broccoli require hours of digestive activity before their vitamins reach your cells. With solid food, we get fibre and although fibre is good, it does slow down the process of digestion. On top of this it tires the whole system and it results in our bodies working hard to assimilate those much-needed miraculous vitamins. I did an experiment some months ago whilst juicing, where I amassed all the solid food I would have eaten and put it in a clear bin bag. The result was over 3.5 kilos of solid food that my body would have had to digest in one day. The body works so hard every day to process all kinds of junk that we put inside of it that it makes sense to give it a break. If you think about it in terms of time, your body takes five–seven hours to digest a bowl of vegetables and fruits whereas it takes just 15 minutes to digest the same ingredients when it's been juiced.

I am not suggesting a diet solely consisting of juices, as that would be completely unhealthy and unsustainable. Instead, I am advocating a balance between drinking vegetable and fruit juices and eating solid meals and snacks. Strive for a balanced, composed and long-term approach to your health.

JUICING & BLENDING

Is it better to use a juicer, which removes the pulp and gives you a very thin consistency juice or blend your vegetables in a blender, so all the fibre remains and you are left with a thicker smoothie?

FRESH RAW JUICES relieve the digestive system of much of the energy required to process the solid food. The nutrients get absorbed into the bloodstream and you will feel the benefits much more quickly.
BLENDED JUICES/SMOOTHIES retain the fibre, which acts as an intestinal sweep and will help your colon remain in constant movement and in health. Some ingredients such as seeds, nut milks, nuts and powders are best used for smoothies (blends).

THE RULE: Drink more juices than smoothies. Both are good for your bodies in different ways. Use your vegetable juice for instant nourishment throughout the day and incorporate smoothies into your diet for a healthy maintenance of your internal systems.

NATURAL & PROCESSED SUGAR

The main thing to remember about sugar is the difference between natural and processed. Natural sugars can be found in vegetables and fruits. Whilst processed sugars are manufactured products, they are created by intense heat and are damaging for your system. Avoid all processed sugars.

But what about the natural ones? The truth is that fruits contain more natural sugars than vegetables, and when we juice fruits they turn into glucose. This is a problem because the fruits have now become sugars (with juice you get no fibre, and fibre slows down the digestive process) and goes straight into your bloodstream which causes insulin spikes. Continuous insulin spikes create stored fats in your body and start causing inflammations and then diseases. Remember it is always better to eat your fruits and drink your vegetables. Fruits eaten, contain the fibre which will slow down the release of sugar into your body, whereas juiced vegetables will release all the goodness and essential missing vitamins quickly back into your body, without insulin spikes.

CRAVINGS

The body is amazing, it knows when to go to sleep, when to wake up and even when to repair itself when it's wounded. Your heart never misses a beat and your lungs are always breathing. So, when you have a craving, something, somewhere is required. A craving is not a weakness, it is an important message to help you find the all important balance. You need to ask yourself, what does my body need and why? Almost 95% of the time the reason for cravings is a lack of nutrients: if the body is depleted from the right nutrients it needs, it will produce cravings for non-nutritional forms of energy, such as sugar.

BALANCE

Balance is a seven letter word, with a deep spiritual meaning and a hard to reach attainable value. It is not easy to be balanced, but it is very important to find an equilibrium when it comes to the food we put into our bodies. Juice diets that last for five, seven or 21 days are too extreme for our bodies and will only cause havoc to our system. Some people may have lost weight on them, but was it weight that they have kept off, or has it crept back into their lives? Diets just don't work. They are too extreme, not long-term orientated and most of the time leave our bodies undernourished. They create unrealistic goals, that are deemed to fail, leaving the dieter unhappy, unworthy and quite simply, sad.

'Balance' offers a sustainable approach to food and health. One juice a day, increases the amount of nutrients in your body, whilst allowing you to go on with your everyday life. Most importantly, one juice a day over a long period of time offers an incomparable injection of health into your body that is approachable, easy and workable.

RAW FOOD

It's time to examine the protagonists of our juices and smoothies: the raw ingredients. Raw and living foods are a clean, simple and controllable source of nutrients and they offer incredible amounts of detoxification, immunity and cleansing. A raw food is an uncooked produce such as vegetable, root, nut, flower, seed and sprout. Live foods contain enzymes which act as catalysts for detoxification and absorption of nutrients.

You don't want to cook anything that goes into your juices or smoothies as you want to preserve the nutritional content of each of your ingredients. Raw foods will give you a different kind of energy and feeling, as they are pure and untouched. Processing and cooking your ingredients takes away most of the pure goodness of your produce, and although it feels natural to cook and eat, it makes sense to start thinking about increasing the percentage of raw food into your daily intake.

FRESHNESS & ORIGIN

Think of where each product has come from. If it is further away than your home country, think of all the travelling, the extreme temperature variances, the extended transit times and the complex logistics it has gone through to reach your supermarket shelf.

THE JUICE INGREDIENTS

When you are juicing, there are some ingredients that you'll use more than others. These specific ingredients will become the central characters of your juice. These ingredients break down into four categories: Vegetables, fruits, spices and herbs.

VEGETABLES

SPINACH is high in vitamins A and K, so it helps maintain healthy eye sight and increases resistance to infection it also helps with blood clotting and bone health.

CELERY is a great source of soluble fibre which helps maintain a healthy digestion as well as being high in vitamin C, which keeps the circulation flowing and lowers the cholesterol.

CARROTS are rich in vitamin A, specifically a form called beta-carotene. They are also full of antioxidants and help maintain a healthy heart. The vitamins from carrots are absorbed better when juiced.

CUCUMBER is great for sustaining hydration due to its high water content. The skin of a cucumber contains silica, which forms the collagen we need to maintain healthy skin and glossy hair.

BEETROOT is high in potassium which helps maintain healthy blood pressure, it also helps to detoxify and cleanse the liver. It has lots of antioxidants and helps prostate cancer.

SWEET POTATO is abundant in vitamin A. It's also key in maintaining a healthy immune system, healthy skin and allowing cells to grow properly.

KALE is one of the best sources of bone-protecting vitamin K which allows the body to properly absorb calcium for strong, healthy bones. It also helps reduce acidity and inflammation externally and internally, whilst detoxifying the body.

FRUITS

APPLE aids the digestion process as it contain lots of enzymes which help break down food and speeds up the metabolism. They are low in fructose and high in vitamin C which helps collagen formation. The skin should always be left on the apple as it contains lots of powerful antioxidants.

PINEAPPLE is a very concentrated source of vitamin C. It is filled with antioxidants, and manganese which helps increase the metabolism.

MELON has a high water concentration so it is very hydrating, as well as being high in vitamins A and C and antioxidants. It also helps fight cardiovascular disease.

LEMON is rich in vitamin C, so it helps us fight off illness. It also helps cleanse the blood due to its high potassium content and it fights off signs of ageing.

SPICES

CAYENNE PEPPER is an anti-inflammatory spice that stimulates the digestion, muscle movement and ensures healthy circulation.

GINGER contains potent anti-inflammatory gingerols which relieve the pain of arthritis, as well as helping with weight loss and helps combat illness.

HERBS

DANDELION is high in vitamins A, C, iron and calcium. It also helps lower cholesterol levels and stimulates the growth of friendly bacteria which is essential for a strong digestion and immune system.

MINT is a calming herb that helps digestion and soothe the insides, as well as being antibacterial, which helps fight off infection.

PARSLEY is high in folate, antioxidants and vitamins C and K which protect the immune system and helps create strong bones.

LEMONGRASS is highly antibacterial and helps remove unwanted bacteria from the digestive system.

INGREDIENT MEASUREMENTS

All the measurements are designed to be home-friendly. Nobody wants to sit at home and weigh their spinach out before juicing it, it's not time-efficient and it's not going to help incorporate juicing into your life! However, I have included more exact weights and measurements, just in case you want to double-check the amounts.

½ HANDFUL - 15G
1 HANDFUL - 30G
2 HANDFULS - 60G

½ CUP - 50G
1 CUP - 100G
2 CUPS - 200G

A SMALL PINCH - ½ TEASPOON
A PINCH - 1 TEASPOON

LEMON JUICE MEASUREMENTS There are two ways of adding your lemon in the juice recipes: if you want your juice to taste really citrusy, juice the lemon in your juicer. If you like your juices more subtle, squeeze the lemon on top of your juice (make sure you cup your hand underneath, to catch any pips).

*All spoons measures are level unless otherwise stated.

ORGANIC

Juicing relies heavily on fresh fruit and vegetables as its core components. However, unfortunately for us juicers, fruits and vegetables are the most pesticide-ridden food produce out there, so it is important to be mindful of the choices we make. As it's expensive to buy everything organic, this section allows you to assess the ingredients that are the most important to buy pesticide-free.

Pesticides pose a real risk to our health. They can cause serious complications and us juicers are exposed to these horrific chemicals, as leafy greens are one of the most pesticide rich produce. Food that is grown without pesticides is really the best diet nourishment you can put into your body. However, there are cost implications with buying organic and sometimes it's not easy to find organic produce without having to spend time getting to the source.

Here is a list of the six dirtiest foods (full of chemicals) and a list of six of the cleanest foods (lowest in pesticides). Write this out and keep it on your fridge or in a small pocket of your bag. When you're next in front of the vegetable and fruit isle in the supermarket I suggest you spend your money going organic on only the most pesticide-ridden fruit and vegetables.

DIRTY LIST
1. Apple
2. Celery
3. Cucumber
4. Spinach
5. Strawberry
6. Kale

CLEAN LIST
1. Papaya
2. Avocado
3. Cabbage
4. Cantaloupe
5. Pineapple
6. Sweet potato

JUICING EQUIPMENT

WHAT JUICER TO BUY?

There are four types of juicers on the market. Centrifugal, masticating, triturating and cold pressed. All four types are different in terms of the end product, price and time allocated to juicing.

CENTRIFUGAL

These machines are the most common and the least expensive. The centrifugal machine throws the vegetable product against a blade, and then strains the juice whilst retaining the pulp (to discard).

PROS Quick to use, easy to clean, low cost.
CONS Less effective in extracting the nutrients from the produce as the pulp remains unused. Inefficient in juicing leafy greens as too much heat is generated and so the juice gets oxidised too quickly with too much foam and not an enough intense flavour.

MASTICATING

These machines grind the vegetables and extract the juices in one much slower step than the centrifugal machine. They chew the produce slowly, hence the word mastication, pushing it through a drill and squeezing out the juice.

PROS The juice is richer in nutrients than a centrifugal juice and it produces a good amount of flavour. Also, not that much heat is involved in the process and you get more juice from your produce. Additionally, you can juice wheatgrass.
CONS Typically more expensive, takes a longer time to juice, more time to prepare the produce and takes a longer time to clean.

TRITURATING

This machine has two interlocking augers (gears) which slowly crush the produce as it passes through them and separates the liquid from the drier pulp.

PROS Can juice any type of vegetable, herb and grass, and produces more juice than your masticating machine. Also, the slower process prevents oxidisation so the juice does last longer.
CONS More expensive and slower than centrifugal and masticating.

If you are a beginner, start by buying a centrifugal juicer. It is a tool that will get you juicing without having to spend too much money.

HYDRAULIC/COLD PRESSED

Most people believe that cold pressed is the same as masticating juicers, but actually they are very different. A cold pressed machine has two separate components and steps to making the juice: a grinder to grind the vegetable into a fine, moist pulp and a cold press to extract the juice from the pulp against two metal plates. There is only one machine in the market that is a cold pressed juicer, and that is the Norwalk, which is what we use in our stores.

PROS Juice produced by this method contains 25 times more nutrients, full flavoured end result. It's a fact that 50% more juice will be produced with the Norwalk than any other machine.
CONS Extremely expensive, very heavy, takes a long time to prepare, juice and clean.

ESSENTIAL TOOLS

1. JUICE EXTRACTOR choose your machine carefully, do your research and read reviews before you buy.
2. LARGE CHOPPING BOARD it's really useful to be able to chop all your vegetables and fruits on the same surface and it also saves both time and cleaning.
3. SIEVE probably the most important tool you need, for when you wash your fresh produce.
4. STANDARD KNIFE don't buy anything special. However, make sure that the piece of steel (the knife blade) doesn't touch your raw ingredients too much.
5. SMALL SCRUB BRUSH for thoroughly washing all vegetables and fruits (especially ones which are not organic).
6. PEELER a home kitchen peeler will do.
7. SET OF PORTABLE SPEAKERS there's nothing better than listening to your favourite music, whilst juicing.
8. GOOD-QUALITY GLASS CONTAINER which fits underneath the funnel of your machine (with an airtight seal).
9. SPATULA you will need this when you are manoeuvring your pulp.
10. STEEL MIXING BOWL
11. THREE KITCHEN CLOTHS to place under your juicer, chopping board and produce, for easy clean up.
12. SPRAY CONTAINER for your wash formula.

PREPPING

You have your tools, you have your knowledge and you have your willingness. Now it's time to start prepping.

No matter how big or small your kitchen is, start by allocating a space for your new juicer. The location is key, as it needs to be accessible. Leaving it in eye sight will get you closer to your goal of incorporating juice into your life. If you put it inside a cupboard, the hassle of taking it out every day is reason enough not to make it a consistent part of your day. Here are some simple tricks to prepping before you start juicing, which will save you time and ultimately make it easier to incorporate juicing into your life.

1.MUSIC have a pair of speakers or a small radio next to your juicer, to motivate you.

2.KEEP THE SPACE CLEAN place one towel under your juicer and one under your chopping board. When you are done, all you need to do is shake the towels and wash them.

3.CHOOSE THE SIZE OF YOUR STEEL MIXING BOWL depending on how much juice you need, you will need to select the correct sized bowl. When you have set up your juicer, take your bowl and head to the fridge. Place your juice ingredients into it and move to the sink for washing.

4.USING BIG BOWLS WILL MAKE YOUR LIFE EASIER as it will save you lots of time walking between your juice station and your fridge. If you have too many ingredients in your bowl, throw them in a sink halfway full of water or if you don't have that many ingredients,

put water in your bowl, and soak them for three minutes.

5.WASHING IS THE MOST IMPORTANT STEP as the taste of your juice will vary massively if you don't wash the produce properly. Take your homemade wash formula (see page 23) or your biodegradable produce wash, and spray your vegetables with it. Quickly scrub them with your brush, rinse them and put them on your chopping board. Wash your ingredients thoroughly if they are not organic, as you need to wash off all pesticides.

6.DECIDE THE SIZE depending on your juicer and its chute, you will need to decide the size you need to chop your ingredients. (The less you use a steel knife, the better, as steel oxidises the produce.)

7.PLACE YOUR GLASS container underneath your juice funnel and turn it on.

CLEANING

This is possibly the only element of juicing, that may irritate you, but here are some time-saving tips that should make your juicing life much easier.

Have you considered juicing at the same time as you are cooking meals? You don't have to separate the two functions – that way the cleaning part is one and the same. Try doing it simultaneously, and use the leftover juice ingredients in a salad or fruit plate. The most important lesson about cleaning: do it straight away.

CLEANING YOUR JUICER
1. Take out the parts of your juicer, stick them in the dishwasher together with your other dishes.
2. Deconstruct the machine, rinse the components under warm water, place them next to the device and leave to dry. This is surprisingly much quicker than the first step.

CLEANING YOUR PRODUCE
If you don't buy organic ingredients it is essential that you thoroughly scrub them with a small scrub brush before you juice them. This will hopefully wash off any residual pesticides on the surface of your fruits and vegetables. You can either use biodegradable produce wash or elect to make your own.

HOMEMADE PRODUCE WASH FORMULA
Mix it all together.

2 lemons
2 tbsp vinegar
1 tbsp bicardonate of soda
Grape seed extract
250ml water

THE JUICES

The juice recipes are separated into three meal time zones: breakfast, lunch and dinner. Certain ingredients are much more useful to our bodies at specific times of the day. However, that doesn't mean you can't mix and match. Experiment with these recipes to make them your own!

All the juice recipes are designed for one person/350ml per glass. Hopefully, this should make it easy for one, but equally if you are making for more than one person or want to store extra in the fridge, all you need to do is multiply your quantities by the amount of glasses you need.

THE BREAKFAST JUICES

The most essential juices are the breakfast juices, as your
body has been resting and fasting for at least eight-nine hours,
so it's literally starving for nutritional goodness. The base
ingredients in all the breakfast juice recipes are green, leafy
vegetables as the health-giving properties in these vegetables
will benefit and stimulate your system throughout the day.

GREEN WAKE UP

KALE FOUNDATION

SPINACH DYNAMO

GREEN POWERHOUSE

HERBAL RETREAT

ALOE VERA HEALER

GREEN WAKE UP

Drink this juice first thing! It really will wake up your system as cucumber is such a strong diuretic. It is also a very hydrating ingredient, so it will give you the much needed goodness your body is craving in the morning.

3 medium-sized cucumbers, unpeeled
a handful of spinach (stalks removed)
1 green apple, unpeeled
a handful of parsley
1 lemon (squeezed or juiced, according to taste, see page 18)

SERVES 1 (350ML)

Always juice the most liquid vegetables first. Start by adding in half your cucumbers, then add your spinach, the rest of your cucumbers, your apple, your parsley and finally your lemon.

Drink immediately or pour into an airtight container and keep in the fridge for up to 12 hours.

KALE FOUNDATION

Kale is the powerhouse of vitamins and that's why it's the main ingredient in this breakfast recipe. Although it's a bit bitter, it tastes incredibly cleansing. It will help combat internal inflammations (which can cause many illnesses) and the glucosinolates in it will add an extra boost of detoxification. Don't forget to layer your vegetables whilst juicing. Mixing the most juicy with the more leafy greens, will get the greatest amount of juice from both.

I medium-sized cucumber, unpeeled
2 handfuls of kale (stalks removed)
I apple, unpeeled
a small handful of mint
I lemon (squeezed or juiced, according to taste, see page 18)

SERVES 1 (350ML)

Start by juicing the cucumber and the kale together and then add your apple, mint and lemon. It's important to always stir your juice whilst you are making it and before you drink it.

Drink immediately or pour into an airtight container and keep in the fridge for up to 12 hours.

TIP
Grate a little lemon zest on top of your glass to finish.

SPINACH DYNAMO

This recipe contains one of the healthiest ingredients, spinach, both for its taste and also for its health benefits. Spinach will cleanse your body if you drink it first thing and it will also stimulate your peristaltic motion. (This is a series of contracting and relaxing nerves and muscles that jump start your internal system.) However, be careful with spinach, if you add too much, the taste will be too bitter and if you add too little, you won't be able to taste it at all.

1 medium-sized cucumber, unpeeled
1 green apple, unpeeled
2 handfuls of spinach (stalks removed)
1 thumb-sized piece of fresh root ginger, unpeeled
a handful of parsley
1 lemon (squeezed or juiced, according to taste, see page 18)
a pinch of cayenne pepper

SERVES 1 (350ML)

Start by juicing the cucumber, apple and spinach together. Then add a small piece of ginger and the parsley and finish it off with lemon. Finally, add a pinch of cayenne pepper on top of the juice, to give it an extra tang.

Drink immediately or pour into an airtight container and keep in the fridge for up to 12 hours.

GREEN POWERHOUSE

Apple is a magnificent fruit. If you start your day with one fruit, let apple be it. It is extremely low in fructose, so it helps slow down the break up of carbohydrates. If you are eating breakfast alongside your juice, add an apple to your juice, as it will help your body manage its blood sugar levels and it will help you feel more balanced throughout the day.

2 green apples, unpeeled
1 celery stick
a thumb-sized piece of fresh
    root ginger, unpeeled
a handful of coriander
1 lemon (squeezed or juiced,
    according to taste, see
    page 18)

SERVES 1 (350ML)

Add your apple, celery, ginger and coriander all together and finish by adding the lemon into your juice.

Drink immediately or pour into an airtight container and keep in the fridge for up to 12 hours.

TIP

Remember to always juice your apples unpeeled. But, please be sure to wash them thoroughly before juicing, especially if they aren't organic.

HERBAL RETREAT

This juice pays homage to herbs! You've got to love a herbal juice not only for its taste, but also because it helps break down the fats formed from our abusive relationships with sugar.

a handful of mint
a handful of Thai basil
a handful of coriander
a handful of tarragon
a thumb-sized piece fresh
   root ginger, unpeeled
3 medium-sized cucumbers,
   unpeeled
I lemon (squeezed or juiced,
   according to taste, see
   page 18)
a pinch of cayenne pepper

SERVES 1 (350ML)

The important thing to remember with this recipe is to juice all the herbs and ginger with the cucumbers. Don't leave the herbs until the end, because they will get stuck in your juicer and go to waste. Add the lemon and a small bit of cayenne pepper to finish.

Drink immediately or pour into an airtight container and keep in the fridge for up to 12 hours.

ALOE VERA HEALER

This recipe focuses on the magical and medicinal plant, aloe vera. If you can, do go out and buy a fresh aloe vera plant as it is sensational. However, if you don't have the time, you can use bottled organic aloe vera as a substitute. This incredible ingredient contains all eight essential amino acids we need, it is high in vitamins and minerals and most importantly it's an adaptogen. (An adaptogen is something that boosts the body's natural ability to adapt to external changes and to resist illness.) It also aids your digestion, detoxification and does wonders for your skin. This is one ingredient you will definitely fall in love with.

4 tsp fresh aloe vera or 4 tsp liquid aloe vera
2 medium-sized cucumbers, unpeeled
a handful of spinach (stalks removed)
I green apple, unpeeled
a handful of coriander
I lemon (squeezed or juiced, according to taste, see page 18)

SERVES 1 [350ML]

Start by scooping the aloe vera from the leaves and putting it through your juicer with one cucumber. (However, if you are using liquid aloe vera, run it through at the end with your last ingredients.) Continue by adding your second cucumber and your spinach and finish off with your apple, coriander and lemon.

Drink immediately or pour into an airtight container and keep in the fridge for up to 12 hours.

THE LUNCH JUICES

Whilst the breakfast juices are mostly vegetable based, the
lunch recipes contain a much greater mixture of greens and
fruits. This is because, just as the breakfast recipes are aimed
at cleansing and injecting nutrients, lunch juices are aimed
towards sustaining your vitality, vigour, energy, regulating the
system and keeping your energy levels up. Lunch juices are an
essential nutrient injection you need in the midst of your busy
day. Although, most people are out of the house at this time, if
you prepare these juices in the morning, you can take them to
work or keep them with you on the go.

The key to a great lunch is to start with a juice and then
continue with a light meal, allowing your body to absorb
the goodness from the juice, followed by the much needed
carbohydrates and protein from the food afterwards.

CARROT ENERGISER

LEAF LUNCH

BEETROOT TONER

LEMONGRASS DE-STRESS

KALE POWER

E3 LIVE JUICE

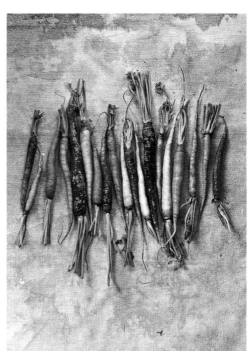

CARROT ENERGISER

A rapid infusion of carrot juice into the system can leave you feeling more energised than drinking an espresso. Carrots help normalise and stabilise our whole system and are the richest vegetable in vitamin A. They help keep our bones and teeth healthy, resist infections and increase our overall vigour and vitality. What else could you want from a midday juice? A lot of people discuss the high sugar content of carrots. These are natural sugars and they absolutely don't pose any adverse risks to our health. In fact, a fresh carrot juice takes away our cravings for really unhealthy, processed sugars.

4 large carrots, peeled
a thumb-sized piece of fresh
    root ginger, unpeeled
a pinch of turmeric

SERVES 1 (350ML)

Juice half the carrots with the ginger, and then add the rest of the carrots. Finally, add a pinch of turmeric on top.

Drink immediately or pour into an airtight container and keep in the fridge for up to 12 hours.

TIP

Usually you should avoid peeling your carrots, instead you should wash and scrub them carefully and intensely, but this is timely.

LEAF LUNCH

This recipe mixes the goodness of carrots with the strength of green, leafy vegetables to make the perfect pit stop lunch juice that will leave you feeling both energised and full.

4 carrots, peeled
2 handfuls of spinach (stalks
    removed)
1 celery stick
a small handful of mint
2 medium-sized cucumbers,
    unpeeled

SERVES 1 (350ML)

Start by juicing the carrots with the spinach. Then add the celery with the mint and finish off with the cucumbers.

Drink immediately or pour into an airtight container and keep in the fridge for up to 12 hours.

To serve, add some ice.

BEETROOT TONER

It's beetroot time! Another restorative ingredient perfect for a lunch juice. Beetroots increase your blood flow by toning your blood and lowering your blood pressure. They have been proven to increase your stamina, which is exactly what you need midday, if you feel that your energy levels are dropping. At the same time, the betalin pigments inside the beetroot help detoxify our livers and break down the toxins that are stored in our bodies.

2 carrots, peeled
1 whole beetroot with
  greens, well scrubbed
  and unpeeled
1 green apple, unpeeled
a handful of watercress

SERVES 1 (350ML)

Never throw away the greens from your fresh beetroot! The green leaves contain so many amazing nutrients and have an intense amount of flavour.

Juice your carrots first, add the beetroot along with its greens and finish off with the apple and watercress. Remember to always stir your juice whilst juicing, because the flavour will be stronger and fuller.

Drink immediately or pour into an airtight container and keep in the fridge for up to 12 hours.

TIP

When you are juicing the beetroot be careful not to wear something you love. If it stains, it won't come off.

LEMONGRASS DE-STRESS

The star ingredient in this juice is lemongrass. Lemongrass contains two polyphenol oils; limonene and citral, which both have antibacterial properties. It's important to feed the body with lemongrass at lunchtime, so it can eliminate and kill all the toxins and bacteria the body has built up. It also has powerful pain-relieving properties, so if you are suffering from a cold or muscle ache this is a great ingredient to add into your juices. Finally, it also has the ability to alleviate stress, so it's beneficial in stress-related conditions (especially in the midst of your busy day).

3 carrots, peeled
3 sticks of lemongrass
2 thumb-sized pieces fresh
   root ginger, unpeeled
1 green apple, unpeeled
a pinch of sea salt

SERVES 1 (350ML)

Start by juicing your carrots and lemongrass, so that you can infuse your main ingredient in the juice from the start. Continue with the ginger and the apple and then add a pinch of sea salt for added flavour.

Drink immediately or pour into an airtight container and keep in the fridge for up to 12 hours.

KALE POWER

Kale is unbelievably good you, it is the queen of vegetables. It is just so perfect for your body and wellbeing at lunchtime. It fills you up and keeps you going sometimes even until dinner.

2 handfuls of kale (stalks removed)
1 ½ medium-sized cucumbers, unpeeled
a handful of coriander
1 celery stick
a tiny piece of jalapeño pepper
1 lime, squeezed

SERVES 1 (350ML)

Start by juicing the kale and the cucumber together. Continue with the coriander and the celery, add the jalapeño. Finish by squeezing the juice of a lime, whilst stirring your juice.

Drink immediately or pour into an airtight container and keep in the fridge for up to 12 hours.

E3 LIVE JUICE

E3 Live is a superfood – a powerful form of algae, which contains over 65 nutrients, amino acids and essential fatty acids. It is a great superfood to keep in your storecupboard and to add into any of your juices and smoothies. This recipe is perfect for lunch, as it contains all you need to keep you energised and strong for the rest of the day, without making you feel lethargic or bloated. This juice will help you repair from within and will keep you coming back for more.

1 tsp E3 Live
½ glass of mineral or filtered water
2 green apples, unpeeled
2 handfuls of spinach (stalks removed)
1 medium-sized cucumber, unpeeled
a handful of mint
1 lime, squeezed

SERVES 1 (350ML)

This is one of the only juices using a powder supplement. The trick with E3 Live is always to add it to half a glass of mineral or filtered water first and stir well. Then juice your apples and spinach, with the cucumber and mint into the glass. Finish by squeezing the juice of a lime, whilst stirring your juice.

Drink immediately or pour into an airtight container and keep in the fridge for up to 12 hours.

TIP

E3 Live is available from Holland & Barrett or any other good-quality health food store.

THE DINNER JUICES

Dinner is an essential time of the day to feed your body nutrition. Simply speaking, the body has been heavily burdened by the food choices you have made, the drinks you have consumed and the snacks you have eaten during the course of the day. Your body at this stage is longing to rest, recoup and restore, before it has to start all over again tomorrow.

This is the time to be careful about what you put into your body and not a time to go without having dinner. You need food to love and nourish yourself. This is the moment where you need to look at your food choices and make sure you are giving your body exactly what you need. Injecting a wide variety of nutrients into your system, will carry it through to the next morning. The important thing to ask yourself is 'Have I given my body the best nourishment at a time when it's working hard to replenish itself for the next day?'

SEA MINERAL SUPPLEMENT

PAPAYA CLEANSER

PINEAPPLE DIGESTIVE

SWEET POTATO WEIGHT LOSS

SLEEP ENHANCING HONEYDEW

'TULSI' BASIL JUICE

SEA MINERAL SUPPLEMENT

This dinner juice contains kelp. Kelp is a gorgeous seaweed found at the bottom of the sea and it contains a myriad of minerals that we can't possibly access unless we eat this ingredient. Indeed, many of us turn to sea minerals in our daily supplements to help us support our complex systems. This fresh ingredient is a rich source of iodine, a mineral that supports us, and keeps our thyroid glands functioning healthily. This recipe is a brilliant dinner juice, as it also helps with weight management by improving our metabolism.

½ handful of fresh kelp (or I tbsp powered kelp)
2 cucumbers, unpeeled
a handful of spinach (stalks removed)
½ handful of parsley
I lemon (squeezed or juiced, according to taste, see page 18)

SERVES 1 (350ML)

Be careful how you juice this ingredient as kelp can be tricky. Mix it with the cucumbers and spinach and make sure you don't leave any behind. Add the parsley and lemon at the end, to ensure a great tangy taste.

Drink immediately or pour into an airtight container and keep in the fridge for up to 12 hours.

TIP
Fresh kelp is available online at JustSeaweed.com and in good organic stores. If you can't get hold of fresh kelp, buy kelp granules and add I tbsp to the top of your juice.

PAPAYA CLEANSER

Papaya is an exotic fruit, with an incredible colour and butter-like consistency, which has a vast array of intense nutritional benefits. It's a healing fruit, very high in antioxidants and it has been proven to heal intestinal and cardiovascular disorders. It's also very useful in digestion as its fibre binds with any bad toxins and keeps them away from our healthy colon cells. Most importantly, papaya contains papain which heals inflammation. This is fantastic as it has been proven that internal inflammations are one of the first causes (not symptoms which come much later) of illnesses. Preventing internal inflammation can help keep your system in peak condition and drinking this juice in the evening ensures that all the goodness from the papaya will stay in the body undisturbed, so that it can do what it is supposed to do, heal.

I green papaya, unripened, peeled and seeds removed
I medium-sized cucumber, unpeeled
I green apple, unpeeled
a handful of mint
I tsp raw honey
I tsp ground cinammon

SERVES 1 (350ML)

Always buy your papayas green and juice them before they have ripened. Don't let them ripen, as most of the the healing benefits are found in its green body. Juice the papaya together with the cucumber and the apple and add the mint at the end. Finish off by adding the raw honey and cinnamon.

Drink immediately or pour into an airtight container and keep in the fridge for up to 12 hours.

PINEAPPLE DIGESTIVE

Another ingredient that you will fall in love whilst juicing is pineapple. Its benefits exceed any expectations and are best saved for dinner so your body can absorb them throughout the night. Pineapple's fame is due to its star ingredient called bromelain. This enzyme digests food by breaking down protein (perfect for a dinner juice recipe) and at the same time it's rich in anti-inflammatory and anticancerous properties. Drunk at dinnertime, pineapples will help you absorb the most important nutrients and will fight the free radicals which destroy your healthy cells.

I small cup of chamomile tea
½ pineapple, peeled
2 handfuls kale (stalks
   removed)
I baby lettuce
a handful of mint

SERVES 1 [350ML]

Before you do anything make a small cup of chamomile tea and set it aside.

The secret to pineapple, is that most of its nutrients hide in its core stem, so make sure you juice the whole fruit with the rest of your ingredients. Mix your pineapple with the kale, then juice your lettuce with your mint. At the end, add the cup of chamomile along with one ice cube, as this will allow it to all come together evenly at one temperature.

Drink immediately or pour into an airtight container and keep in the fridge for up to 12 hours.

SWEET POTATO WEIGHT LOSS

You might find the addition of sweet potato in a juice a bit peculiar, but it's perfect for a dinner juice because although it's filling it's also very nutritious. It's a wealthy source of beta-carotene (which is a powerful antioxidant) and it contains vitamin B6 which will keep your heart healthy. In the meantime, this ingredient is perfect if you are trying to cut down on carbohydrates, lose weight or gain muscle. This is undoubtedly a nutritional powerhouse of a juice!

1 sweet potato, peeled
2 medium-sized cucumbers, unpeeled
1 green apple, peeled
a thumb-sized piece of fresh root ginger
1 lemongrass stick

SERVES 1 (350ML)

Start by juicing your sweet potato and one cucumber, then add the apple and ginger together with the lemongrass, and finish off with your last cucumber. Don't forget to stir it continually.

Drink immediately or pour into an airtight container and keep in the fridge for up to 12 hours.

SLEEP ENHANCING HONEYDEW

This juice recipe is sweet enough to replace any dessert. As well as being sweet, it has a vast amount of vitamin C in it (the juice of a honeydew provides 35% of the daily recommended dosage our body needs). It also prepares us for a good night's rest, with an incredible amount of hydration for our skin. Enjoy!

1 medium-sized cucumber, unpeeled
1 handful of spinach (stalks removed)
½ small honeydew melon, rind removed
½ handful of coriander
1 stick of lemongrass

SERVES 1 (350ML)

Start juicing your cucumber with the spinach. Then add the honeydew and the herbs.

Drink immediately or pour into an airtight container and keep in the fridge for up to 12 hours.

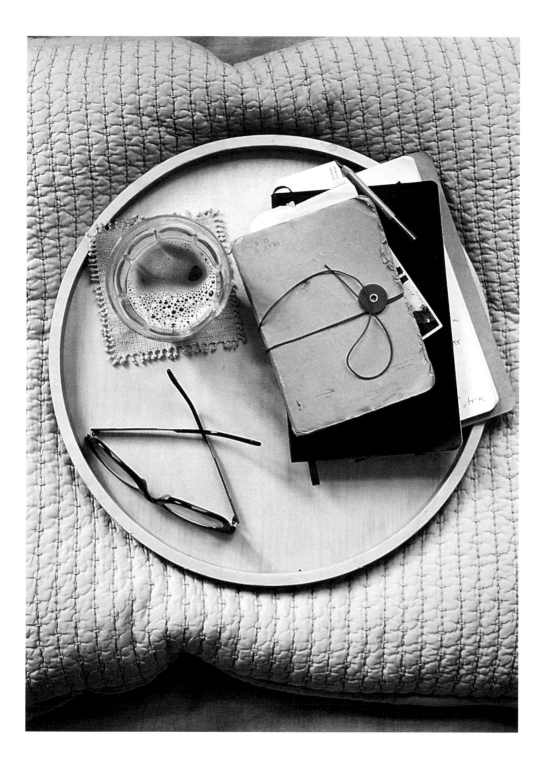

'TULSI' BASIL JUICE

Tulsi, otherwise called India's 'Queen of Herbs', has so many nutritional benefits. One of the most important facts is that the 'Holy Basil' can really help relieve symptoms of a cold, such as fever and the shakes. It purifies your blood, and it helps alleviate stress whilst it is proven that in homeopathic treatments, if drunk daily for six months it can eliminate kidney stones naturally. This beautiful herb will enhance your overall wellbeing, while keeping you calm and peaceful.

2 medium-sized cucumbers, unpeeled
a handful of tulsi or basil
I red apple, unpeeled
I tsp fresh aloe vera or bottled aloe vera juice

SERVES 1 (350ML)

A great way to start juicing this recipe, is to wash and chew four–five tulsi (or basil) leaves. The taste will liven up your palette and prepare it for the juice. Mix your cucumbers with your tulsi (or basil), add your apple and then the aloe vera and stir.

Drink immediately or pour into an airtight container and keep in the fridge for up to 12 hours.

TIP
If you can't get hold of tulsi, substitute it for basil, it is still fantastically good for you.

THE TARGET JUICES

These juices have been designed to target specific parts of your body, system or wellbeing, as the ingredients within them have been scientifically proven to aid their targeted causes. These juices are ideally drunk when you want to target a particular aspect of your daily life.

* Drink all these juices immediately or pour into an airtight container and keep in the fridge for up to 12 hours.

STRENGTH

ACTIVE

WEIGHT LOSS

GLOWING SKIN

DE-STRESS

SHINE FROM THE INSIDE

STRENGTH

SERVES 1 (250-300ML)

2 carrots, peeled | ½ whole beetroot
with greens, well scrubbed and peeled
a handful of kale (stalks removed)
1 green apple, unpeeled | 1 lemon
(see page 18) | a pinch of turmeric

Start by juicing your carrots, beetroot and kale and
then continue with your apple. To finish off squeeze
the lemon and add a pinch of turmeric.

ACTIVE

SERVES 1 [250-300ML]

3 large slices of watermelon, rind removed | a handful of mint

Juice half of your watermelon, add your mint in the middle and then add the rest of the watermelon. Whilst making this juice, chew some mint leaves, they will prepare your body and taste buds for what is coming.

WEIGHT LOSS

SERVES 1 (250-300ML)

2 large slices of watermelon, rind removed | 1 carrot, peeled | a thumb-sized piece of fresh root ginger, unpeeled | 1 slice of honeydew melon, rind removed | 1 lemon (see page 18) ½ tsp cayenne pepper

Juice your watermelon, with your carrot and ginger and the honeydew melon. Finish off by squeezing the lemon and sprinkling with a little bit of cayenne pepper!

GLOWING SKIN

I tsp chia seeds | I tbsp fresh or
bottled aloe vera | I orange, peeled
I medium-sized cucumber, unpeeled

SERVES 1 [250-300ML]

Place the chia seeds in the base of your bowl so
they can soak up the juice. Pour the fresh or bottled
aloe vera on top, and then juice the orange and
cucumber to finish off.

73

DE-STRESS

SERVES 1 (250-300ML)

250ml fresh coconut water | I green apple, unpeeled | ½ tsp ground cinnamon

SERVES 1 (250-300ML)

Pour the coconut water into your glass and then add your juiced apple on top and stir. To finish, add a pinch of cinnamon. (Please try and use juice from a fresh, young coconut, it will transform the flavour of the juice!)

SHINE FROM THE INSIDE SERVES 1 (250-300ML)

½ medium-sized cucumber, unpeeled | 1 green pepper | 1 tbsp fresh or bottled aloe vera | 1 green apple, unpeeled

If you are using fresh aloe vera, juice your cucumber, pepper, aloe vera and apple together and enjoy. If you are using bottled aloe vera, add it to the base of your glass and then pour your juice over it.

THE SHOTS

THE SHOTS

Shots are ideally drunk in the morning, before your first juice,
but they actually do work equally well when drunk at any point
of the day. Due to their potency and concentrated ingredients
they are perfect if you need a direct energy pick-me-up or even
if you feel unwell and want an injection of healing nutrients
straight into your system. They are super-easy to make, as
they don't contain many ingredients and are designed for seven
specific purposes.

* Drink all these juices immediately or pour into an airtight
container and keep in the fridge for up to 12 hours.

CLEANSE

CLEANSE+

DETOXIFICATION

ENERGY

REDUCING INFLAMMATION

OXYGENATING

ANTIBACTERIAL

HEALING

CLEANSE

a thumb-sized piece of fresh root
ginger, unpeeled | 1 lime | ½ lemon
a pinch of cayenne pepper

MAKES 1 SHOT

Juice all together and mix well.

CLEANSE+

1 slice of honeydew, rind removed
a handful of coriander | 1 lime
½ handful of dandelions (or herb
equivalent i.e. Thai basil, tarragon,
coriander and mint)

MAKES 1 SHOT

Juice all together and mix well.

DETOXIFICATION

MAKES 1 SHOT

a handful of dandelions (or Thai basil, tarragon, coriander and mint) | a thumb-sized piece of fresh root ginger, unpeeled | a pinch of cayenne pepper

Juice the dandelions (or herbs) and the ginger together and add the pepper at the end.

ENERGY

½ medium-sized cucumber, unpeeled
1 tsp maca powder | ½ tsp raw cacao
powder

Juice the cucumber and then blend it in a blender with
the maca and the cacao powder.

REDUCING INFLAMMATION MAKES 1 SHOT

½ medium-sized cucumber, unpeeled
100g alfalfa sprouts

Juice both the cucumber and the alfalfa sprouts.
Mix well.

OXYGENATING

4 handfuls of wheatgrass

MAKES 1 SHOT

Juice and drink up.

ANTIBACTERIAL

MAKES 1 SHOT

I green apple, unpeeled | I tsp
fresh oregano

Juice the apple and add the oregano on top.

HEALING

MAKES 1 SHOT

½ green papaya, unripened, peeled and deseeded | 1 tsp fresh or bottled aloe vera

Whilst you juice the papaya, add the aloe vera through your juicer so it comes out in one shot and has a unified taste.

JUICING+

JUICING+: THE BASICS

This section of the book is all about mantaining your healthy
lifestyle alongside your juices. Obviously juices are extremely
important, but it's also vital that they are consumed alongside
smoothies, infused waters, milks and butters. It is all about
finding the right **PURE** 'balance'.

The most exciting part of adopting the juicing lifestyle is how
often you will find new ways of adding healthy ingredients into
your diet. **Juicing+** is all about beginning to find and add new,
amazing superfood ingredients into your daily regime which will
further enhance your energy and existence.

Eating healthily is something that needs to happen every day
and it takes a lot of effort and a re-alignment of your mindset to
begin with. But ultimately, it gives you back the most precious
present: a life full of energy, stamina and happiness without
ailments and obstacles, so you can really achieve exactly what
you want out of life.

THE JUICING+ INGREDIENTS

FRUITS

AVOCADO is rich in fats, but because they are monounsaturated they have plenty of benefits, not least for the cardiovascular system. Avocado is also rich in vitamin B5, which plays an important role in generating energy from food. B5 is also required to support our adrenal output, which is incredibly useful in times of stress. Despite the fat content, avocado can also help reduce our cholesterol as it contains its own sterols that block absorption of the unwanted form.

BLUEBERRIES are notable for their anthocyanin content, a plant pigment that gives them their blue-purply colour. These have powerful antioxidant properties but they offer many other antioxidant nutrients as well including resveratrol, often cited as the reason why red wine is a healthier choice, then white. Blueberries are remarkably useful and research suggests that they can have a wide range of benefits from reducing muscle soreness after exercise to improving cognitive function when juiced.

DATES are a rich source of vitamins and minerals, whilst providing plenty of fibre. They are completely free from cholesterol and contain very little fat, whilst being high in antioxidant vitamins A and C. They are also rich in potassium, which is critical in managing our body's salt and water content. This is particularly important in our modern day diets which are high in processed foods that contain a lot of salt. All sugars are completely natural, so the body is able to digest more of them and use them for energy – however, don't have too many as too much of any sugar isn't good for you.

SUPERFOODS

ACAI is a small purple berry which comes from the acai tree in Brazil. High in antioxidants, Acai berries help protect against heart disease, arthritis and premature ageing. They have a great blend of omega 3 and 6 (the same as olive oil), which is important for our cardiovascular health. They are also high in fibre that is key to maintaining a healthy digestion and lowering our cholesterol.

BEE POLLEN is made by honeybees and contains nearly all nutrients required by humans. It is high in protein at 40% as well as amino acids, vitamins, including

B-complex, and folic acid. Bee pollen helps reduce levels of histamine which helps hay fever sufferers, its anti-inflammatory properties aid breathing and it helps with both immunity and energy levels.

CACAO NIBS have the same nutritional benefits as cacao powder (as it's still a raw product). However, the difference is that these tasty little nibs have a great texture and add a crunch to your smoothie, whilst still being really good for you.

CHIA SEEDS are South American seeds which were used as a currency by the Aztecs, now they are used as a protein, calcium, vitamin and fibre rich superfood. The omega 3 content in chia seeds has been associated with the cellular health of our brain and has been associated with giving relief for people suffering from depression. The mix of B vitamins is key in converting food to energy and helping muscles work properly – so they're very important for anyone who likes to exercise, whilst the incredibly high calcium content is important for bone health.

GOJI BERRIES contain all essential amino acids, vitamin C, 21 trace minerals and are high in fibre. They have 15 times the amount of iron found in spinach, as well as calcium and zinc; they give bone, brain and cell strength. They are filled with antioxidants and also have compounds rich in vitamin A that protect against skin damage and benefits the immune system.

MACA is a Peruvian plant that Inca warriors used to give them strength before battle. The main benefit of maca is that it is a carbohydrate, which is a vital energy source for active people; it helps with growth, repair and endurance. It also has a high iron content, which helps combat anaemia, important for anyone on a low-meat diet. Additionally, its high vitamin C count helps heal wounds and supports the immune system, whilst also being an antioxidant which fights off free radicals.

RAW HONEY is honey that has not been heated, pasteurised or processed in any way. It contains antibacterial and antifungal properties, whilst being highly alkaline, which neutralises the acidity in our bodies. It promotes digestive health and is a powerful antioxidant, strengthens the immune system, eliminates allergies and is an excellent remedy for skin wounds and infections. Raw honey can also stabilise blood pressure, balance sugar levels, relieve pain, calm nerves and it has been used to treat ulcers.

POWDERS

LUCUMA POWDER is a fruit known to have been eaten by the Incas. It has a delicious, sweet caramel flavour, whilst being equally high in antioxidants, fibre and vitamin A. Fibre helps lower cholesterol and stabilises our blood sugar as well as aiding our digestion. Lucuma is great as it's easily digested whilst still giving the benefits of fibre. It's high in antioxidant vitamin A which we need for eye sight as well as reproduction of cells and a strong immune system.

RAW CACAO POWDER not to be confused with cocoa, it's the raw, uncooked base for chocolate manufacture and is packed with antioxidants that neutralise free radicals and prevents cell damage. These antioxidants also help metabolise sugar, avoiding issues with high blood pressure and diabetes. Almost 50% of cacao's mass is made up of three types of fat, none of which are harmful to us. Oleic acid is the fat found in olive oil, a monounsaturated fat that the body breaks down easily, and the others stearic and palmitic acids are believed not to build cholesterol. Additionally, cacao contains a lot of magnesium which is critical to our nervous health, a lack can lead to increased stress.

SUPER-GREEN POWDERS are typically made up of wheatgrass, barley, grass and spirulina, all of which are high in chlorophyll (the dark green pigment that gives plant's their colour). Chlorophyll is a superfood that gives us energy and detoxifies our bodies whilst being a powerful antioxidant that protects us from inflammation, bad skin and aids our digestion. It also provides us with magnesium, vitamin K, vitamins B and C, folic acid, iron, calcium and protein which helps build, repair and maintain our muscle tissue. The high number of amino acids found in these super-green powders, is particularly important to anyone who follows a plant-based diet, as they often lack these acids in their diets.

PROTEIN SUPPLEMENTS

HEMP PROTEIN is a great alternative for anyone who is intolerant to lactose or glucose. It has a range of phytonutrients (nutrients from plants) and is a rare food that provides all 20 amino acids, so it's a great way for vegetarians or vegans to get their daily dose. It's high in zinc which is critical for brain function and has been closely linked to high cognitive ability. Its high protein content is one of the reasons it's becoming increasingly popular with sports people (50% of its mass is in fact protein).

WHEY PROTEIN is the protein contained in whey, the watery portion of milk that separates from the curds when making cheese. It is used for improving athletic performance as it is a great source of protein which regulates our weight and increases our muscle mass.

EQUIPMENT FOR JUICING+

Juicing+ requires some basic equipment that will give you an incredible variety to your daily diet. If you decided to buy the equipment for the Juicing section, you will already own a sieve, a knife, a chopping board, a steel mixing bowl and a spatula. So, the only remaining pieces of equipment you need are:

A BLENDER

You probably already own a blender at home. But for nut butters, you will need a strong, durable machine which can grind nuts, fruits and vegetables to a puréed or ground consistency. As you will be making nut milks, butters and incredible smoothies, you do need to use a machine that's powerful and durable. It's important that you don't go for the cheapest gadget on the market, as the process will take longer and will ultimately make you feel demotivated. Go for power, quality and most importantly, stainles-steel blades or grinders. Think about investing in something that will last a long time, with a guarantee, which will ultimately take the hassle out of blending your raw ingredients.

NUT MILK BAG OR MUSLIN

To strain and make your nut milks.

COLANDER

To strain your agua frescas/smoothies bases.

JAM JARS

To store your homemade nut butters in.

THE SMOOTHIES

THE SMOOTHIES

SMOOTHIES HAVE THREE LAYERS:
1. A base
2. Fruit and/or vegetables
3. Superfoods, seeds and rest of ingredients

THE CHOICE OF BASES:
Homemade juice (see pages 28-75)
Agua fresca (see pages 116-123)
Nut milk (see pages 126-129)
Fresh coconut water

THE ALL-DAY BREAKFAST

THE BIG BOY

THE BEE

THE GYM FREAK

THE COCONUT HYDRATOR

THE SMART ONE

THE ULTIMATE CHOCOLATE SMOOTHIE

THE AGUA FRUIT SMOOTHIE

THE ALL-DAY BREAKFAST

This is an essential morning smoothie, as it contains raw oats. Remember how good it is to eat your food in its original, raw form? The oats will keep you going until lunchtime, and you won't crave anything unnecessary during the day. Added to which, the seeds contain lots of protein and the cacao nibs are packed full of antioxidants, both of which you need to kick-start your day.

230ml homemade almond milk (see page 127)
1 banana, peeled
3 tbsp oats
1 tbsp almond butter (see page 132)
2 tbsp sesame seeds
1 tbsp cacao nibs

SERVES 2 (250ML EACH)

Blend all your ingredients together.

THE BIG BOY

This is an ideal meal replacement drink for when you are on the go. The combination of seeds will give you the perfect amount of essential fats and the cacao powder will help metabolise all the bad sugars your body contains. Even the blueberries will give you the perfect brain boost for when you need it the most!

230ml homemade almond milk (see page 127)
1 tsp organic vanilla extract or small piece of vanilla pod
1 tbsp Mixed Nut Butter (see page 132)
1 tbsp cacao powder
10–12 blueberries
1 banana, peeled
1 tsp oats
1 tbsp flaxseeds
1 tbsp pumpkin seeds

SERVES 2 (250ML EACH)

Blend all your ingredients together.

THE BEE

Honestly, this smoothie is a godsend. The bee pollen contains nearly all the nutrients we need and it's high in protein, amino acids and vitamins (it's the most important superfood). The raw honey will neutralise the acidity in your body and the dates will help balance your body's salt/water ratio and most importantly will give you tons of energy all day!

230ml almond milk (see page 127)
1 banana, peeled
½ tsp bee pollen
1 tsp raw honey
2 dates, stones removed
2 tsp sesame seeds
a pinch of ground cinnamon

SERVES 2 (250ML EACH)

Blend all your ingredients together.

THE GYM FREAK

By far one of the most popular smoothies at Roots & Bulbs, The Gym Freak does exactly what it says: it gives you energy pre- or post-work out. The Chocolate Hazelnut Butter will give you the right amount of fats (remember some fats are good). The hemp protein powder will give you all of your 20 amino acids and the maca will boost your endurance levels whilst you are working out!

250ml Vanilla Almond Milk (see page 127)
1 banana, peeled
½ tsp homemade peanut butter (see page 132)
½ tsp Chocolate Hazelnut Butter (see page 133)
1 tsp hemp protein powder
1 tsp maca powder
1 tsp cacao nibs
2 tsp sesame seeds

SERVES 2 (250ML EACH)

Blend all your ingredients together.

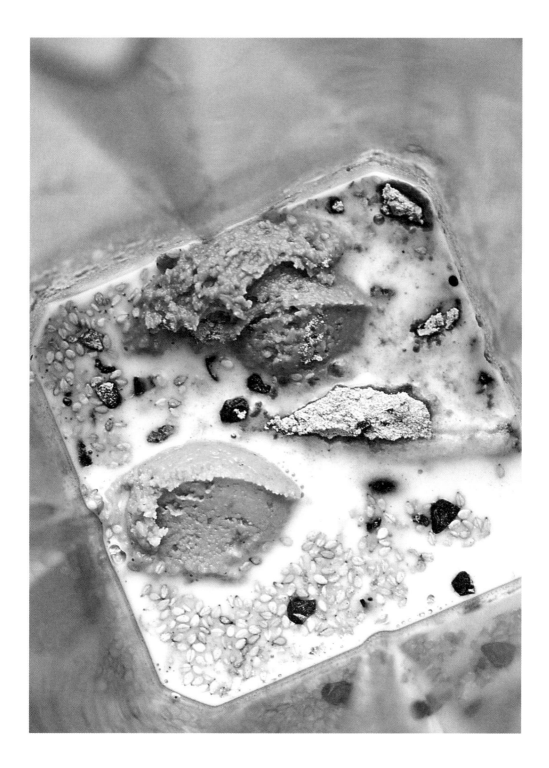

THE COCONUT HYDRATOR

When you are feeling extremely dehydrated and need a strong dose of electrolytes into your system, this smoothie is the go-to smoothie of choice. Ideal for a snack or for after a work out, this smoothie will heal you from the inside, when you need a helping hand. It's also perfect for boosting skin and hair growth.

280ml fresh coconut water, plus all meat from coconut
1 tsp spirulina
1 tsp chia seeds

SERVES 2 (250ML EACH)

Blend all your ingredients together.

TIP
Please try and buy a young Thai coconut, cut it open; use the water and the flesh. The taste will be infinitely better than packaged coconut water, which will have been pasteurised.

THE SMART ONE

This smoothie is designed as a pick-me-up for when you are feeling tired or mentally exhausted. It contains coffee and coffee beans, which makes it a smart alternative to a single shot of coffee, which will leave you lethargic and hungry! The fresh coconut water will hydrate your body, the walnuts will give you essential nutrients to help carry you through your day and the coffee beans will give some bite to your smoothie!

230ml coconut water, plus
   I tsp coconut meat
I banana, peeled
I tsp raw cacao powder
5 walnuts, shelled
2 dates, stones removed
I single espresso shot
I tsp coffee beans

SERVES 2 (250ML EACH)

Blend all your ingredients together.

THE ULTIMATE CHOCOLATE SMOOTHIE

Perfect for your heart and in times of stress, the avocado in this smoothie makes it the creamiest and healthiest chocolate snack you will ever have. The rest of the ingredients will fill your body with goodness and health. Incredible for a snack or a meal replacement, this smoothie is highly addictive!

230ml almond milk (see
   page 127)
1 whole avocado, peeled
100ml fresh coconut water
1 tsp raw cacao powder
1 tsp sesame seeds

SERVES 2 [250ML EACH]

Blend all your ingredients together.

THE AGUA FRUIT SMOOTHIE

If you want some more fruit in your smoothie, this recipe is extremely refreshing on a summer's day. The key to this smoothie is the combination of fruit, superfoods and spice!

250ml Watermelon Base
  (see page 103)
3 ripe strawberries
1 banana, peeled
a handful of mint
1 tsp chia seeds
a pinch of ground cinnamon

SERVES 2 (250ML EACH)

Blend all your ingredients together.

THE AGUA FRESCAS /
SMOOTHIE BASES

These agua frescas (often called infused waters) are the base for
smoothies, and are fresh, nutritious and tasty. They are also a
refreshing way to make your smoothies more flavoursome.

Remember that although these are meant to be bases for your
smoothies, there is no reason why you can't drink them on their
own, after you have chilled them in the fridge!

* Drink all these agua frescas immediately or pour into an
airtight container and keep in the fridge for up to two days.

ORANGE & GINGER BASE

WATERMELON BASE

BERRY BASE

BERRY BASE | ORANGE & GINGER BASE

WATERMELON BASE

ORANGE & GINGER BASE

3 organic oranges, peeled
   and deseeded
2 thumb-sized pieces of
   fresh root ginger, unpeeled
2 limes
1 litre filtered or mineral
   water

SERVES 4 (1 LITRE)

Peel your oranges and cut them into cubes ensuring
they are seedless. Place into the base of a jug. Then,
add both the ginger and lime and mash the ingredients
together with a spatula. Once thoroughly mixed, add
filtered or mineral water.

Leave the water to sit in the fridge completely covered
for 2 hours.

Then, strain the agua fresca with a colander (so some
seeds are left in the water) before you drink, or before
you add to a smoothie.

WATERMELON BASE

3 slices watermelon, rind
    removed
a handful of mint
a handful of basil
3 tbsp raw honey
1 litre filtered or mineral
    water

SERVES 4 (1 LITRE)

Peel your watermelon and cut into cubes ensuring
they are seedless. Place them into the base of a jug.
Then, add the mint, basil and raw honey and mash the
ingredients with your spatula. Once thoroughly mixed,
add filtered or mineral water.

Leave the water to sit in the fridge completely covered
for 2 hours.

Then, strain the agua fresca with a colander (so some
seeds are left in the water) before you drink, or before
you add to a smoothie.

BERRY BASE

600g raspberries,
   strawberries and
   blackberries
I litre filtered or mineral
   water

SERVES 4 (1 LITRE)

Wash your mixture of raspberries, strawberries and blackberries. Place into the base of your jug. Then, mash the ingredients with your spatula. Once thoroughly mixed, add filtered or mineral water.

Leave the water to sit in the fridge completely covered for 2 hours.

Then, strain the agua fresca with a colander (so some seeds are left in the water) before you drink, or before you add to a smoothie.

TIP

These agua frescas
should be drunk
within two days
of making.

THE NUT MILKS &
THE NUT BUTTERS

THE NUT MILKS

Nut milks are so easy to make and incredibly nutritious. They add a rich and creamy texture to your smoothies and they contain protein and essential fats, that will keep you energised whilst you strive to pack as much as possible into your day.

Although, you will find lots of packaged nut milks in the supermarket, they contain lots of sugars and additives to extend their shelf life and make them taste better. So that's why it's super important to try and make your own. Although, it takes longer, it is so much healthier for you and the end result tastes incredible.

We often have customers who come into our stores and ask if we have a secret ingredient we add into our smoothies. They say that they try to replicate them at home and they taste nothing like ours. When we ask them what type of nut milk they use for their drinks, they say they use packaged nut milks from the supermarket. That is exactly why ours taste better, and why yours will too. Make your own nut milks. It is completely worth it.

PREPARING THE NUT MILK

- Soak 300g nuts (almonds, cashews, brazil nuts, hazelnuts or hemp seeds) overnight at room temperature in salted water. Don't soak for over 12 hours (cashew nuts only require two hours soaking).

- Drain the nuts or the seeds and throw away the now dirty soaking water.

- Place the swollen nuts into your blender with a litre of filtered or mineral water.

- Blend for about a minute. When you see the nut mixture become smoother and form a white creamy surface, they are ready to be strained.

- Place the nut milk bag inside your metal bowl, hold both sides of the bag and carefully begin to pour the liquid into it.

- You will start seeing your gorgeous milk coming out of the bag into the metal bowl. Start slowly twisting your bag so that you can squeeze all the milk that is leftover in the pulp of your nuts or seeds.

- Place in an airtight container straightaway and store in the fridge for three days. You should have almost a litre of milk. This amounts to three smoothies, and a bit of milk for your coffee. You can also use the milks for your cereal and even for your porridge.

GREEN TEA ALMOND MILK

250ml almond milk (see page 127)
Add ½ tsp organic green tea matcha powder
a pinch of ground cinnamon

SERVES 1 (250ML)

Pour your almond milk into a blender.
Then, add your organic green tea matcha
powder and cinnamon. Blend thoroughly.

VANILLA ALMOND MILK

250ml almond milk (see page 127)
1 vanilla pod (or 4 drops of vanilla extract)
2 dates, stones removed
a pinch of ground cinnamon

SERVES 1 (250ML)

Pour your almond milk into a blender,
with 1 vanilla pod (or 4 drops of vanilla
extract). Then add the dates and a pinch
of cinnamon. Blend thoroughly.

CHOCOLATE HAZELNUT MILK

250ml hazelnut milk (see page 127)
½ tsp raw cacao powder
½ tsp vanilla extract
½ tsp cacao nibs

SERVES 1 [250ML]

Pour your hazelnut milk into a blender and add your raw cacao powder, vanilla extract and cacao nibs. Blend thoroughly.

CINNAMON CASHEW MILK

250ml cashew milk (see page 127)
2 dates, stones removed
a pinch of ground cinnamon
1 tsp raw honey

SERVES 1 [250ML]

Pour your cashew milk into a blender along with the dates, cinnamon and raw honey. Blend thoroughly.

THE NUT BUTTERS

Nut butters should be used all the time in smoothie making, as they provide essential fats and flavour. They change the whole consistency of the smoothie into a creamy, delightful drink with some bite.

Making your own nut butter ensures that you will always know exactly what has been added to your smoothies. Your nut butters will never include additives, stabilisers and sugars that supermarket butters contain to extend their shelf life. These homemade butters are the real thing, only containing ingredients that will provide your body with the best nutrition.

These homemade nut butters will keep for a maximum of 10 days, but they are so delicious they will be long finished before their 10-day expiry date.

MIXED NUT BUTTER

CHOCOLATE HAZELNUT BUTTER

MIXED NUT BUTTER

100g almonds
50g cashews
50g pecans
50g walnuts, shelled
1 tsp coconut oil
4 dates, stones removed
1 tbsp ground cinnamon

MAKES 150G

Blend all the nuts together for three minutes until they are all smooth. Then, add your coconut oil, dates and cinnamon

Continue to blend for a further eight minutes on a slow and steady pace until the texture is soft and creamy. Put in an airtight container and close the lid. Store at room temperature for a maximum of 10 days.

TIP

If you want to make one pure nut butter, replace the weight of the other nuts with your single choice of nut (250g). Peanut and almond butters are fantastic!

CHOCOLATE HAZELNUT BUTTER

300g hazelnuts, shelled
1 tsp coconut oil
3 tsp raw cacao powder
  (untreated and
  unprocessed)
2 tsp cacao nibs

MAKES 150G

Blend the hazelnuts and coconut oil slowly for three minutes. Then, add your raw cacao powder and cacao nibs.

Continue to blend for a further eight minutes on a slow and steady pace until the texture is soft and creamy. Put in an airtight container and close the lid. Store at room temperature for a maximum of 10 days.

JUICING JARGON

FIBRE is an important part of a healthy diet and helps prevent heart disease, diabetes, weight gain, some cancers and can also improve digestive health. There are two different types of fibre – soluble and insoluble. Each type of fibre helps your body in different ways, so a healthy diet should include both types. Soluble fibre can be digested by your body and can help reduce cholesterol. Foods that contain soluble fibre include: oats, barley, rye, bananas, apples, carrots and potatoes. Insoluble fibre can't be digested. It passes through your gut without being broken down and helps other foods move through your digestive system more easily. Insoluble fibre keeps your bowels healthy and helps prevent digestive problems. Good sources of insoluble fibre include: wholemeal bread, bran, nuts and seeds. Whilst juicing, insoluble fibre is removed so that the nutrients are more readily absorbed as the digestive system doesn't have to separate them from the fibre.

ENZYMES are large proteins that act as catalysts to help speed up digestion and break down foods. There are different types of enzymes, some are specifically for fats, carbohydrates and proteins. Digestive enzymes are needed to help break down foods so that your gut can distribute the nutrients from food. The number of enzymes that we can produce is limited, which is why it's so important to have the right foods that contain these. Both, fruit and vegetables are high in natural enzymes.

ANTIOXIDANTS are man-made or natural substances that may prevent cell damage, caused by an overload of free radicals. Free radicals are caused by an increase of toxins in the body from things such as such as pollution, cigarette smoking, alcohol, sunlight and heavily processed foods. Antioxidants are found in many foods, including fruits and vegetables and specifically in foods that contain vitamins A, C and E. There is good evidence that eating a diet with lots of vegetables and fruits is healthier and lowers your risk of certain diseases.

GLUCOSE is a simple sugar and carbohydrate that comes from food and is essential in the body for all cells and organs. It gives us energy, and without it we wouldn't be able to live. When we eat food, it is broken down into sugar in our stomachs and then absorbed into the bloodstream. Glucose is stored as glycogen in our liver, to be used when we need energy. If we have too much, the glucose is eventually stored as fat so it is essential to have it as part of a balanced diet and to get our glucose from healthy sources such as fruit and vegetables.

FRUCTOSE often referred to as fruit sugar, is found in fruits, honey and to a lesser extent, in vegetables. It is often thought of in positive terms as it is a 'natural' sugar because it comes from fruit. Small doses of fructose are acceptable for the body, however, it shouldn't be consumed in large doses and only in its natural form (from fruits and some vegetables). It's often found in large amounts of heavily refined, processed foods, sweets and fizzy drinks, and the negative effects of this can include liver damage, increased fat storage and overeating due to its addictive nature.

VITAMINS are substances that your body needs to grow and develop normally. There are 13 vitamins your body needs. They are vitamin A, B vitamins (thiamine, riboflavin, niacin, pantothenic acid, biotin, vitamin B6, vitamin B12 and folate), vitamin C, vitamin D, vitamin E and vitamin K. Your body can also make vitamins D and K. People who eat a vegetarian diet may need to take a vitamin B12 supplement. Vitamins A, C, E are also antioxidants to help to protect the body from free radicals. Vitamins B and C are water-soluble which means that we lose them daily through bodily processes such as sweat and urination so they must be replaced. Fat soluble vitamins A, D, E and K are stored in the liver, and to get the full benefits of these vitamins they are best absorbed with some healthy fats such as avocado or olive oil (uncooked). The best way to get vitamins is to eat a varied diet that is not processed. Many processed foods extract vitamins to increase their shelf life.

AMINO ACIDS are chains of chemicals that join together to make proteins. Protein is essential for growth and repair in the body. There are 20 amino acids that combine to make different proteins, and humans can produce 10 of the 20 amino acids. The others must be supplied in the food. Amino acids must be taken daily as the body does not store them.

MINERALS are an essential part of a healthy diet. Your body uses minerals for building bones, making hormones and regulating your heartbeat. There are two kinds of minerals: macrominerals and trace minerals. Macrominerals are minerals your body needs in larger amounts. However, your body needs just small amounts of trace minerals. Minerals are found in foods such as meat, fish, milk and dairy foods, vegetables (particularly dark green, leafy vegetables), fruit, beans and nuts. You can get all of the minerals that you need from a plant-based diet, vegetables are an excellent source.

FREE RADICALS are highly unstable molecules and can be formed when oxygen interacts with certain molecules. They are formed from a variety of conditions including when our body is exposed to toxins in our environment, sunlight, cigarette smoke, alcohol and the food that we eat (processed, fried foods are the worst). Once a free radical is formed, it turns other molecules in the body into free radicals. Oxidative stress is brought on by free radicals and is thought to play a role in a variety of diseases including cancer, cardiovascular diseases, diabetes, Alzheimer's disease, Parkinson's disease and eye diseases. To prevent the effects of free radicals it is key to have a diet high in antioxidants.

PULP is the part of vegetables and fruit that contains the fibre. When juicing, the pulp is extracted from the vegetables and fruit in order to remove the insoluble fibre. Often when juicing using a traditional juicer with a blade there is still pulp left, which is wet. Twice cold-pressed juice is free of pulp – it's the purest form of the juice – and the nutrients are easily absorbed as they have been freed from the fibre.

SPIRULINA is a type of blue-green algae that is rich in protein, vitamins, minerals, carotenoids and antioxidants that can help protect cells from damage. It contains nutrients, including B-complex vitamins, beta-carotene, vitamin E, manganese, zinc, copper, iron, selenium, and gamma linolenic acid (an essential fatty acid). Studies suggest that spirulina may boost the immune system, help protect against allergic reactions and have antiviral and anticancer properties.

WHEATGRASS is grown from the wheat seed (wheat berries), which is the whole kernel of the wheat grain. It is a healing grass and one of the best natural sources of vitamins A and C. It's a great purifier of the stomach, liver, pancreas and circulatory system. When juiced it is a powerful, raw food with over 80 enzymes. It has been known to help speed up metabolism, detox the body, help the digestive system, develop a healthy immune system and aid glowing skin.

THE JUICE PLAN

The Juice Plan is a gentle cleanse, but one with a difference. It's a reboot that's been devised to deliver concentrated levels of nutrients along with some fibre, fat and protein, all of which our bodies need to function on an everyday basis.

This cleanse is different to typical cleanses because it's a short term plan (one–two days maximum) and because it contains other nutritional elements such as almond milk and nuts. Adding almond milk, will offer you protein which stabilises your blood glucose levels and chewing the nuts will communicate to your brain that you are still eating, which is super important when you are hungry and craving food.

The Juice Plan shouldn't cut your calories to a level were you feel horrible, instead it should offer a practical short-term focus that gives your body a break, together with the nutrients it needs.

BREAKFAST	500ml Green Wake Up (see page 28) + one handful of nuts
MID A.M.	250ml almond milk (see page 127)
LUNCH	500ml Kale Foundation (see page 30) + one handful of nuts
MID P.M.	250ml almond milk (see page 127)
LATE AFTERNOON	500ml Kale Foundation (see page 30) + one handful of nuts
EVENING	500ml Green Wake Up (see page 28) + one handful of nuts
LATER	500ml Kale Foundation (see page 30)

MOTIVATION

More than anything, I believe in a sustainable approach to eating. Nothing works better, than when you approach your diet with a consistent and balanced point of view. When I started juicing, I would never have got better, if I had expected to see immediate results. We live in a world that is so fast-paced and immediate, that we all want immediate gratification and instant results. Unfortunately, our bodies don't work this way – they need time to heal and restart.

My juicing experience has helped me to get to where I am today, healthy, revived and more energetic than ever and I hope I have motivated you to do it too. It takes a lot of will-power to stay attached to your juicing beliefs and to stick to juicing every day, whilst continually eating healthier food. I did not opt for a juice diet to get instant results, I knew I needed a long-term plan. I practised discipline and self-love, two very difficult attributes, so that I could reach my goal. I knew deep inside, that juicing would work, because all the nutritional facts made sense. There are no fads, no lies and no false claims – just the truth: Drinking vegetable juices will heal my body from within.

It worked – it took a year until I started feeling better, but I got there. And that feeling of achievement is one I will never forget, it's what keeps me going, every dark, gloomy London morning, when I have to make my green juice so that I can maintain the incredible feeling of clarity and energy that juicing provides me with.

There will come a time, after you have juiced for a while, where you feel demotivated. I know how much easier it will seem to opt for a snack rather than making your juice. I urge you to not give up! I urge you to trust in me and believe that you will achieve all you want, by drinking small quantities of juice every day. If you get fed up with repetitive juicing, mix it up with shots, target juices, smoothies and even start creating your own juices with your favourite ingredients. Don't stop, just when your body is starting to appreciate all the goodness you are feeding it. Don't give up, because that feeling of achievement you will gain when you reach your goal, is incomparable!

We have reached the end of our juicing journey together. Whilst writing this book, I have fallen in love with juicing all over again! I feel incredibly lucky that I have been given the chance to write about something I love so much, and I am so grateful to have had you onboard with me throughout.

I 100% believe in every word I have written here, and I hope you now do too.

All my love,
Sarah

ROOTS & BULBS

Publishing Director Jane O'Shea
Creative Director Helen Lewis
Editor Romilly Morgan
Designers Gemma Hogan, Emily Lapworth
Photographer Kristin Perers
Prop Stylist Holly Bruce
Food Stylist Camilla Baynham
Production Vincent Smith, Stephen Lang

First published in 2015 by
Quadrille Publishing Ltd
Pentagon House
52-54 Southwark Street
London SE1 1UN
www.quadrille.co.uk

Text © 2015 Sarah Cadji
Photography © 2015 Kristin Perers
Design and layout © 2015 Quadrille
Publishing Limited

Cataloguing in Publication Data: a catalogue record for this book is available from the British Library.

ISBN: 978 184949 575 2

Printed in China

INDEX

ACKNOWLEDGEMENTS

I would have never been able to complete this book without the support, love and constant attention from my husband, Laurent. He kept me going, when it all got too much, and carried me when I felt overwhelmed and overworked. The incredible love that he gives me every day, has allowed me to open my heart and pour it into this book. I dedicate it to him and to our little girl who is coming into this world in less than 10 weeks.

My editor, Romilly Morgan has been so supportive and lovely along the way and I wish to thank her for her openness and extremely kind way of handling me throughout the process. I would also like to thank Rachael for her hard work and help in writing the book.

Kristin Perers, the most incredible photographer I have come across. This book would never have looked as good without your magic touch.

Most importantly, I thank you for buying this book and for believing in me and what I have to say.